AF270186

ACTS

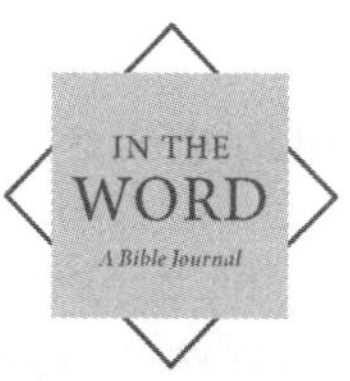

ACTS

Rob Wynalda, Joel R. Beeke,
and Paul M. Smalley

REFORMATION HERITAGE BOOKS

Grand Rapids, Michigan

Reformation Heritage Books
3070 29th St. SE
Grand Rapids, MI 49512
616-977-0889
orders@heritagebooks.org
www.heritagebooks.org

25 26 27 28 29 30/11 10 9 8 7 6 5 4 3 2

ISBN 979-8-88686-167-9

PREFACE

In Deuteronomy 17, Moses leaves final instructions concerning the future of Israel. As a prophet of God, he foretells that Israel will set a king over the nation (v. 14). This king must be an Israelite, not a foreigner (v. 15), and is forbidden to do certain things (vv. 16–17). In verse 18, Moses transitions to what the king should do. The king is commanded not to simply acquire a copy of the law (the entire book of Deuteronomy), but to handwrite his own copy of the law. The purpose was so that he would read it, fear the Lord, obey, avoid pride, not deviate, and enjoy a long reign (vv. 19–20; cf. Prov. 4:20–27).

More than three thousand years later, modern educators have discovered that students who write out notes by hand have a much higher retention rate than those who simply hear or visually read the information. Apparently, God knew this to be true for the kings of Israel also.

This series of books, known as The Bible Journal, was born from the insight found in Deuteronomy 17:18. Your Bible Journal gives you the opportunity to write out your own copy of a portion of the Holy Scriptures, just as the ancient kings of Israel were instructed to do. Writing out the words of the Bible helps a person to engage the Word of God by slowing down the process of reading the text. Writing answers to the discussion questions also helps you to thoughtfully engage the text. Furthermore, by completing a journal, you leave a legacy to pass on to future generations your insights and personal applications of the text (Deut. 6:6–9; Ps. 78:4–7).

To prepare you to meditate on this portion of the Holy Scriptures, we include an introduction to the book of the Bible to help you understand more thoroughly the Bible book you are about to write out in full. Study Questions and Devotional Reflections have been added after the blank pages set aside for copying each chapter of God's Word. The Study Questions focus on individual verses to keep you thinking about what you are writing, and the Devotional Reflections are designed to help you focus on a few of the major takeaways for your practical Christian life that each Bible chapter provides. We wish to thank Reformation Heritage Books for allowing us to use material drawn from *The Reformation Heritage KJV Study Bible* for the Bible Introduction material and for the Devotional Reflections. The Study Questions have been written by the authors of *The Bible Journal*. Thus, The Bible Journal walks you through a process of getting acquainted with a book of the Bible, copying a chapter by hand, reflecting on the meaning and application of that chapter, and then repeating the process for the next chapter. Families, friends, and small groups can work through a journal together, discussing their meditations for mutual edification as guided by the discussion questions.

The mass production of the Bible since the invention of the printing press has greatly blessed the world. However, there is also great benefit for Bible readers of all ages in following the Deuteronomy 17:18 principle and producing your own handwritten copy of the text.

May God richly bless you in writing and learning His Word through The Bible Journal (Rom. 1:16).

—Rob Wynalda, Joel R. Beeke, and Paul M. Smalley

Introduction to the Book of
ACTS

AUTHORSHIP: The author of Acts is the same as that of the Gospel of Luke, as its opening words prove: "The former treatise have I made, O Theophilus, of all that Jesus began both to do and teach" (1:1). Both Luke and Acts are addressed to Theophilus (Luke 1:3). Acts refers to the "former treatise" and continues the record of the work of Jesus from heaven by His Spirit through His apostles. The Gospel of Luke ends with Jesus ascending to heaven and the disciples praising and blessing God in the temple (Luke 24:53). Acts opens with a restatement of Jesus's ascension (Acts 1:9), the same command Jesus gave to His disciples (vv. 4, 12), and the promise of the coming Spirit (v. 5). Likewise, Jesus is the central character of both Luke and Acts, though in Acts Jesus works through His apostles while He is in His heavenly session at God's right hand. These connections between the ending of Luke and the beginning of Acts establish unequivocally the common themes and authorship of Luke over both his Gospel and Acts. Beyond this, the external and internal evidence points to Luke as the common author of both volumes.

We know that the author of Acts was a traveling companion of Paul because of the many "we" statements used in the later narratives (16:10–17; 20:5–15; 21:1–18; 27:1–28:16). We further know that the author was not a companion of Jesus during His earthly life (Luke 1:1–4). Thus the possibilities narrow; we do know that Luke was a traveling companion of Paul (Col. 4:14; 2 Tim. 4:11; Philemon 24). The difficulty and eloquence of the Greek in both Luke and Acts point to a well-educated author who has a knowledge of God's redemptive work throughout the Old Testament, though commentators note that there are many stylistic differences between the two books. Still Luke, a physician, fits the criterion of being such a learned and skilled author (Col. 4:14).

Likewise, external testimony is virtually unanimous in agreeing to Luke's authorship. By AD 200 Luke was the accepted author of both the Gospel and Acts. There are references throughout church history confirming this accreditation. Testimonies from Justin Martyr, the *Muratorian Canon*, Irenaeus, Clement of Alexandria, Tertullian, and Origen all reflect the early church's conviction that Luke is the author.

DATE: The date of Acts is tied closely to the date of Luke. It is almost a universal opinion that Acts was written after the Gospel of Luke. It is believed that Luke was written in the early 60s, and thus Acts would have been written at a later date. It is important to note what events Luke does not include in Acts and to ask why he has left out several important historical occurrences. Looking at these criteria will help us ascertain a close approximation of the date of Acts.

Luke records Paul's preaching before Felix (ruled c. AD 52–60) and Festus (ruled c. AD 60–62) and his imprisonment in Rome, which occurred in AD 62 (Acts 28:11–31). But Luke does not record Paul's release from prison, and there is no mention of Paul's death (likely in AD 67). Likewise, Luke does not record the persecution the early Christians suffered under Emperor Nero (ruled AD 54–68) and includes no hint of the Jewish war in the late 60s. It is important to consider as well that Luke does not include the destruction of the temple in AD 70—a monumental event in both redemptive history and the life of the church. While some scholars argue that Luke left out these important events because they did not fit his purposes in writing, it seems best to conclude that Luke composed Acts somewhere in the early to mid-60s.

THEME: Christ's continuing work after His ascension to expand His church through the gospel preaching of the apostles and disciples throughout the world.

PURPOSE: As with the Gospel of Luke, to confirm the faith of those instructed in Christianity (Luke 1:4) and, further, to deepen that faith by tracing Christ's building of the church from Jewish Jerusalem to Gentile Rome.

SYNOPSIS
The Contribution of the Book of Acts to Redemptive Revelation
Acts is important to the New Testament canon because it carries on the narrative of Jesus's work through His disciples. Acts is not so much about the work of the disciples as it is about the continuing work of Christ from His heavenly session. Acts reveals that Jesus, now seated in glory, continues His work of redemption through His Spirit and for His church. As such, the book gives us a unique glimpse into the life of the early church and the early missionary movements as the apostles took the Word of Christ to the ends of the world.

The Gospel of Luke emphasized the mighty work of God in history through the person and work of Jesus. The Gospel ended and Acts began with the ascension of Jesus to His heavenly throne. But God's mighty act of salvation did not stop with Jesus's ascension. Rather, the ascended Christ now works mightily and savingly through His church on earth. Acts is a record of Christ's continued work in and through His apostles, disciples, and people.

Central to the book of Acts is the manifestation of Christ as the glorious and exalted God over the whole world. Luke uses specific Christological titles to magnify Christ in His exaltation. Christ is the promised Lord and Christ (2:36); He is the appointed Judge of the living and the dead (10:42); He is the greater Son of David (2:30), the promised Messiah (5:42); and He is standing at the right hand of the Father (7:56). Christ's work on earth may be finished, but His work from His exalted state is not. It is in the name of Jesus that the sick are healed (3:6), and His name is the only means of salvation (4:12). It was necessary for Christ to ascend to heaven that He might carry on His ministry even while exalted in glory. Jesus's ascension to God's right hand and the subsequent coming of the Spirit serve as proofs to Jesus's claim of divinity. The Father was pleased with the work of the Son and honored the Son by sending the promised Spirit (5:30–32).

Closely related to Christ's exaltation is the connected note that Christ does not work alone. After He ascended into heaven He sent His Holy Spirit to continue the work Jesus had begun in His disciples (1:8; 2:30–36; 16:7). The Holy Spirit first fell on the disciples (2:1–4), then on the Samaritans (8:17), then on the Gentiles (10:46), and then the disciples of John (19:6). Each of these successive fallings of the Spirit is similar to the initial falling at Pentecost and shows that through Christ's ascended work by means of His Spirit the doors of salvation are equally open to *all* kinds of people to come to Him in faith. Thus the Spirit works as evidence of Christ's power through His disciples to perform signs, wonders, and miracles testifying to His heavenly commission (19:10–11).

A broader purpose is served by Acts as well, that of showing the consequences of the large-scale rejection of Jesus during His ministry and the post-Pentecost inclusion of the nations into the fold of salvation. Acts serves as a major transition in redemptive history, tracing the history of the beginnings of the early church through Paul's final days. Now, as Acts records for us, those who confess faith in Christ and are united to the church become the true possessors of God's covenantal promises. By faith even Gentiles are grafted into God's wonderful plan of redemption and salvation. Acts 1:8 serves as an organizing principle in understanding the gospel development in the book of Acts. Jesus tells His apostles that they will be His witnesses beginning in Jerusalem and extending to Judaea, Samaria, and into the uttermost parts of the earth. As Luke composes Acts he follows this trajectory. The apostles first proclaim the message of Christ's resurrection in Jerusalem (ch. 2). Philip preaches to the Samaritans (ch. 8). An Ethiopian eunuch comes to faith in Christ (ch. 8). And Paul travels to Ephesus and other parts of Asia Minor and Europe, even bringing the message of salvation to Rome. Following this structure Luke shows us the triumph of the gospel and the power of the preached Word as it goes forth converting and turning the world upside down.

OUTLINE

I. The Prologue (1:1–5)
   A. Introduction to Theophilus (1:1)
   B. Summary of Jesus's Final Days on Earth (1:2–3)
   C. Jesus's Final Commands to the Disciples (1:4–5)

II. The Outpouring of the Spirit of Christ (1:6–2:13)
   A. The Ascension of Christ (1:6–11)
   B. The Praying Church (1:12–26)
   C. The Coming of the Holy Spirit (2:1–13)

III. The Increase of the Word (2:14–20:38)
   A. In Jerusalem (2:14–6:7)
      1. Peter's First Sermon (2:14–36)
      2. The First Converts Repent and Are Baptized (2:37–41)
      3. The Unity of the Early Church (2:42–47)
      4. The Healing of the Lame Beggar (3:1–26)
      5. Peter and John Arrested (4:1–22)
      6. The Church Prays for Strength (4:23–31)
      7. Unity and Discipline in the Early Church (4:32–5:11)
      8. Miracles Performed in the Early Church (5:12–16)
      9. The Apostles Suffer Persecution (5:17–42)
     10. Deacons Appointed to Help the Elders (6:1–7)

   B. In Judaea, Galilee, and Samaria (6:8–9:31)
      1. Stephen's Martyrdom (6:8–7:60)
      2. Saul's Persecution Introduced (8:1–3)

C. Paul before Leaders (25:1–26:32)
   1. Paul Appeals to Caesar (25:1–12)
   2. Festus Seeks Agrippa's Advice (25:13–27)
   3. Paul Preaches before Agrippa (26:1–32)

D. Paul Travels to Rome (27:1–28:31)
   1. Paul Sets Sail for Rome (27:1–12)
   2. Paul's Ship Is Wrecked in a Storm (27:13–44)
   3. Paul on the Island of Malta (28:1–10)
   4. Paul in Rome (28:11–31)

Notes

1

2

3

4

5

6

7

Notes

8

9

10

11

12

Notes

13

14

15

16

17

18

Notes

19

20

21

22

23

24

25

Notes

26

STUDY QUESTIONS

1. Verses 1–2: What did Luke write to Theophilus in his former book?

2. Verse 3: How did Christ convince them of His resurrection?

3. Verse 8: What did Christ promise? How does this verse compare to Luke 24:46–49?

4. Verses 9–11: How will Jesus return?

5. Verses 16–18: Who was Judas (Luke 6:13–16)? What happened to him?

6. Verse 20: Read Psalm 69:25 in context. How was this fulfilled in Judas?

7. Verses 21–22: What does this say about an apostle?

8. Verse 24: What attribute of God encourages us to ask Him for guidance?

DEVOTIONAL REFLECTIONS

1. Luke refers to his Gospel as what Jesus "began both to do and teach" (v. 1). The implication is that Christ is continuing to act and teach, now as the Lord enthroned in heaven (v. 9) who works through His Spirit (v. 8). How does the knowledge that Jesus continues to act and teach in the world strengthen the faith of believers?

2. The disciples did not wait passively for the coming of the Spirit, doing nothing, but they devoted themselves to prayer meetings (v. 14). They loved the Scriptures as the infallible voice of God's Spirit (v. 16) and applied the Word to order the church according to God's will (v. 20). Thus they provide an example of how believers should wait for the coming of Christ: by devoting themselves to prayer, the Word, and the church, as ordered by Scripture.

3. Christ captured the mission of the church in the phrase "witnesses unto me" (v. 8). Witnesses do not invent their own message but faithfully declare what they know to be true. The witness of the church did not end with the apostles but must continue to the ends of the earth, for God's purpose is to bring this message concerning Christ and redemption to all nations. Only when all the elect from all tribes and tongues are brought in through the word of Christ's witnesses will the end come. How is your church engaged in this witness? If you are a Christian, how are you part of this mission?

Notes

1

2

3

4

5

6

7

8

Notes

24

9

10

11

12

13

14

15

16

Notes

17

18

19

20

21

22

Notes

23

24

25

26

27

28

29

Notes

30

31

32

33

34

35

36

Notes

37

38

39

40

41

42

43

Notes

44

45

46

47

STUDY QUESTIONS

1. Verse 1: What is the feast of Pentecost (Lev. 23:9–21)?

2. Verse 3: Why did the Spirit come with the sign of fire (Gen. 15:17; Ex. 3:2, 13:21; Luke 3:16)?

3. Verses 4–8: How was Pentecost a reversal of God's work at the tower of Babel (Genesis 11)?

4. Verse 11: What does the Spirit move men to do (Eph. 5:18–19)?

5. Verse 15: The third hour of the day is 9 a.m. Why did Peter mention the time?

6. Verses 17–18: How did Peter explain these events at Pentecost?

7. Verse 21: What is the promise of the gospel?

8. Verses 22–23: How was God at work in the life and death of Jesus?

9. Verses 24–28: Why was it impossible for death to hold on to Christ?

10. Verses 29–31: Why did Peter say that David wrote about Christ, not about David?

11. Verse 33: What happened in heaven that explains the events on earth at Pentecost?

12. Verse 37: How did Peter's preaching affect them?
Why (John 16:7–11)?

13. Verses 38–39: What is the promise to them, their children, and those far off?

14. Verse 42: What characterized the members of this church?

15. Verses 43–47: What extraordinary events were taking place by God's power?

DEVOTIONAL REFLECTIONS

1. The work of the triune God is obvious at every important point of history: creation, incarnation, resurrection, and also Pentecost. Exalted by the Father (v. 33), Christ poured out His Spirit (v. 33), and the Spirit testified of Christ (v. 31) while the Lord added to the church (v. 47). Blessed be the triune God (Eph. 1:3).

2. True repentance for sin and a crying out to God for mercy (vv. 37–38) is the only proper response to the preaching of the Word of God. Never doubt the power of God to convert sinners. He cut the people of Jerusalem to the heart and transformed cowardly Peter into a fearless preacher. Have you come before God as a sinner, seeking mercy for Christ's sake?

3. The church after Pentecost was marked by faithfulness, fellowship, fear, and fervency. Trace this out in verses 41 to 47 and ask whether these qualities characterize you. How can you pray regularly for these characteristics to increase in your own church?

1

2

3

4

5

6

7

8

Notes

9

10

11

12

13

14

Notes

15

16

17

18

19

20

21

Notes

22

23

24

25

26

STUDY QUESTIONS

1. Verse 2: What was this man's hopeless and helpless condition?

2. Verse 6: What did Peter mean, "in the name of Jesus Christ"?

3. Verse 8: What did God's mercy move this man to do?

4. Verse 12: What did *not* cause this miracle?

5. Verses 13–15: What did Peter say about God and Jesus? What did he say about the Jews to whom he spoke?

6. Verse 16: What did cause the miracle?

7. Verse 19: What command does the gospel place upon people? What is its promise?

8. Verses 22–23: What office of Christ was announced here?

9. Verses 25–26: How is God's promise to Abraham fulfilled in Christ (Gen. 12:3; 22:18)?

DEVOTIONAL REFLECTIONS

1. Though the Bible calls Christians to show generosity to the poor, the preaching of the gospel and the transformation that it brings must always be central to the life of the church. Peter used this miracle as an opportunity to declare the power of the name of Jesus, not just to heal the sick but as the person in whom we must place our faith. It is fitting that this miracle took place at the gate called Beautiful, for it reveals the loveliness of the Savior as He takes hopeless sinners and restores them to strength, joy, and praise.

2. Just because God raised Christ from the dead does not mean that people are automatically saved. The gospel calls sinners to repent and be converted so that their sins might be blotted out (v. 19). Do not rest simply on hearing the truth of the gospel, being a child of believers, or being around people who know the gospel. Apart from repentance toward God and faith in the Lord Jesus you are neither saved nor safe. Have you repented?

Notes

1

2

3

4

5

6

7

8

Notes

9

10

11

12

13

14

Notes

15

16

17

18

19

20

21

22

Notes

23

24

25

26

27

28

Notes

29

30

31

32

33

34

Notes

35

36

37

STUDY QUESTIONS

1. Verses 1–2: Why would the Sadducees be grieved that the apostles preached the resurrection (Luke 20:27)?

2. Verse 4: How many men were in the church in Jerusalem at this point? How much had the church grown (Acts 1:15; 2:41)?

3. Verse 8: How did Peter have such boldness (v. 13) to preach as he did?

4. Verses 11–12: What did Peter say about Christ? About salvation?

5. Verse 13: What did they notice about Peter and John?

6. Verses 18–19: What did the council command Peter and John? How did they respond?

7. Verse 24: How did the church respond to persecution?

8. Verses 25-27: How was Psalm 2 fulfilled in Jesus Christ?

9. Verse 28: How was God involved in Christ's death? How would knowing that have given the early church confidence to face opposition?

10. Verses 29–31: What did they pray? How did God answer?

11. Verses 32–35: How was God's power evident in the church?

12. Verses 36–37: What was Barnabas's character?

DEVOTIONAL REFLECTIONS

1. It is often asserted today that people can be saved apart from knowing about Jesus. Some say that explicit knowledge about Jesus is not necessary in order to be saved. Verse 12 stands in absolute contrast to this. We need to be prepared to stand and say this against the tide of relativism in our culture. Why is faith in Jesus Christ the only way to God?

2. The apostles quoted Psalm 2 in their prayer (vv. 25–26). They were bringing back to God His own Word. How does this help us see the connection between these two means of grace: prayer and Bible reading?

3. Though they responded resolutely to the intimidation of the Sanhedrin, the apostles still felt the need to pray to God to grant them "boldness." They were not content to move forward in their own strength or on the strength of past resolutions. They understood their need to draw down strength from God. Do you know this strengthening power of prayer in your life? How dependent are you on God's Spirit?

Notes

1

2

3

4

5

6

7

8

Notes

9

10

11

12

13

14

15

Notes

16

17

18

19

20

21

22

Notes

23

24

25

26

27

28

29

Notes

30

31

32

33

34

35

36

Notes

37

38

39

40

41

42

STUDY QUESTIONS

1. Verses 3–4: How does this show us the Holy Spirit is God and is personal?

2. Verse 5: What happened to Ananias? Why (v. 4)?

3. Verse 8: Why might Sapphira have lied about the price of the land?

4. Verse 11: What did God's judgments on hypocrites produce?

5. Verses 12–16: How did God show that His power was with His church?

6. Verse 19: What does this show us about the power of angels (Acts 12:7–10, 23)?

7. Verse 20: Why did the angel release the apostles?

8. Verses 23–24: How do you think the soldiers and priests felt? What was God showing them (v. 39)?

9. Verses 27–29: What does this teach us about obedience to human authorities?

10. Verse 31: Where do repentance and forgiveness come from?

11. Verse 32: What does this teach us about the work of the Holy Spirit?

12. Verse 34: Who was Gamaliel (Acts 22:3)?

13. Verses 38–39: What was Gamaliel's argument to leave the apostles alone?

14. Verses 40–42: How did the apostles respond to being beaten for Christ?

DEVOTIONAL REFLECTIONS

1. Satan wages war at the level of our hearts, seeking to fill the thoughts and affections of people with greed, deceit, and hypocrisy (v. 3). Yet sinners cannot excuse themselves by saying that the Devil made them do it. Ananias and Sapphira "conceived this thing" in their hearts (v. 4). As a result God rightly judged them for putting on a false show of righteousness. How should this event teach us to fear the Lord?

2. The apostles preached "the words of...life" (v. 20). The message of the gospel is powerful, saving, and effectual when blessed by the Holy Spirit. God uses preaching to bring the spiritually dead soul to life and to increase Christ's life in the believing soul. How should this affect the way we come to read or hear the Word? How should this motivate us to speak it to others who do not yet believe?

3. We naturally shrink back from suffering, and nowhere does the Bible tell us to choose suffering for its own sake. However, if doing the right thing brings suffering, we should not shrink back but learn from the apostles to see our suffering as a privilege in light of God's purpose (v. 41). Why did they rejoice?

Notes

1

2

3

4

5

6

Notes

7

8

9

10

11

12

13

Notes

14

15

STUDY QUESTIONS

1. Verse 1: Why might complaints about Greek and Hebrew-speaking widows produce trouble in the church?

2. Verses 2, 4: What were the apostles' priorities? What does that teach us about pastors today?

3. Verses 3, 5: What kind of people did they appoint to oversee the ministry of mercy?

4. Verses 10–13: How does the world sometimes react to powerful Christian witness?

5. Verse 15: To what does Luke compare Stephen's face? What does that suggest about him (Ex. 34:29; Matt. 17:2)?

DEVOTIONAL REFLECTIONS

1. The apostles discerned the temptation we all face to be distracted from our main callings. Satan bombards us with distractions because he knows we will be far less effective if we are preoccupied with many other things. Every Christian needs wisdom from God to discern his calling so that he can devote himself to it with dedication. Pastors in particular need humility and wisdom to delegate tasks to others. What can you do to be more focused on your calling?

2. What a mercy it was that "a great company of the priests were obedient to the faith" (v. 7). They had served and ministered in the types and shadows of the old sanctuary. But now, not only had the physical veil been torn but the spiritual veil over their hearts had also been rent, and by faith they submitted to the righteousness of God in Jesus Christ. Why was their conversion a surprise (4:1–2)? How does it demonstrate the power of Christ?

3. Stephen was "full of faith and of the Holy Ghost" (v. 5). Though the Holy Spirit is a gift of God, the Bible does command us to seek after the Spirit's work (Luke 11:13) and not to quench (1 Thess. 5:19) or grieve Him (Eph. 4:30). Why do we need the Spirit?

Notes

1

2

3

4

5

6

7

Notes

8

9

10

11

12

13

14

Notes

15

16

17

18

19

20

21

22

23

Notes

24

25

26

27

28

29

30

31

Notes

32

33

34

35

36

37

Notes

38

39

40

41

42

43

Notes

44

45

46

47

48

49

50

Notes

51

52

53

54

55

56

57

Notes

58

59

60

STUDY QUESTIONS

1. Verse 2: What is the Lord called here (cf. v. 55)?

2. Verses 2–8: What did Stephen say about God's promises
   to Abraham?

3. Verses 9–14: What happened to Joseph? How did it
   foreshadow Christ?

4. Verses 15–16: Where was Jacob buried? Why might he have
   desired that?

5. Verse 17: How was God keeping His promise to Abraham while
   Israel was in Egypt (Gen. 17:2; 22:17)?

6. Verse 20: Why did Stephen preach so much about Moses
   (Acts 6:11, 14)?

7. Verses 21–22: What privileges did Moses enjoy as a young man in
   Egypt? How does that highlight his faith when he chose to iden-
   tify with Israel (Heb. 11:24–26)?

8. Verse 24: Why did Moses kill the Egyptian?

9. Verses 25–28: How did the people of Israel respond to Moses at
   this point in his life? How did Moses foreshadow Christ (vv. 35, 39)?

10. Verses 32–33: How do we see again that the Lord is "the God
    of glory" (v. 2)?

11. Verse 34: What attributes of God do we see here (Ex. 3:7–8)?

12. Verse 37: What did Moses predict (Deut. 18:15)? How was that
    fulfilled in Christ?

13. Verses 38–41: How did Israel respond to God's word
    through Moses?

14. Verse 42: What does it mean that God "gave them up"
    (Ps. 81:11–12; Rom. 1:24, 26, 28)?

15. Verses 44–47: On what does Stephen now focus? Why
    (Acts 6:13–14)?

16. Verses 48–50: How did Stephen rebuke the people's attitude to
    the temple (Isa. 66:1–2)?

17. Verse 51: How were the unbelieving Jews of Stephen's generation like their forefathers? What does this mean?

18. Verse 54: How did Stephen's words affect them? How did they respond? How does this compare to the effect of Peter's sermon at Pentecost (Acts 2:37)?

19. Verses 55–56: What did Stephen see and say about Jesus (Ps. 110:1; Dan. 7:13–14)?

20. Verses 59–60: How did Stephen die like Christ (Luke 23:34, 46)?

DEVOTIONAL REFLECTIONS

1. Note that Stephen opens his speech saying, "The God of glory appeared unto our father Abraham" (v. 2). Likewise his speech ends by noting that he "saw the glory of God, and Jesus standing on the right hand of God" (v. 55). Stephen's eyes have been opened to the glory of God in the face of Jesus Christ, as revealed throughout Scripture. What does it mean to read the Bible in such a way as to see God's glory in the face of Christ?

2. Spiritual privileges do not necessarily equate to spiritual possession. Israel was privileged in many ways. When they considered this the equivalent of being God's special possession they deceived themselves, and God punished them by giving them up to idolatry (v. 42). Though they had the Word of God and the external form of His worship, they were "uncircumcised in heart and ears" (v. 51). How should this danger move us to pray for God's work within our hearts?

Notes

1

2

3

4

5

6

7

Notes

8

9

10

11

12

13

14

15

Notes

16

17

18

19

20

21

22

23

Notes

24

25

26

27

28

29

30

Notes

31

32

33

34

35

36

37

Notes

38

39

40

STUDY QUESTIONS

1. Verses 1–4: Who consented to Stephen's death? How did he persecute the church? What was the effect of that persecution?

2. Verses 5–6: What is significant about Philip evangelizing Samaria (John 4:9)? Why did they listen to Philip?

3. Verse 9: What was unusual about Simon? What does the Bible say about this practice (Deut. 18:9–14)?

4. Verse 12: What topics were the subject of Philip's preaching?

5. Verse 14: Why did the apostles send Peter and John to the Samaritans?

6. Verses 15–17: What did Peter and John do for the believers in Samaria? Why was it unusual for believers to need this (Acts 2:38; 1 Cor. 12:12–13)?

7. Verses 18–23: What do Simon's actions show about his spiritual state? How is this possible if he believed and was baptized?

8. Verse 25: What did Peter and John do on their way back to Jerusalem?

9. Verses 26–27: To what place and person did the angel send Philip?

10. Verse 29: Who is the Lord of evangelism and missions (Acts 10:19–20; 13:2, 4)?

11. Verses 30–35: What passage of Scripture was the eunuch reading? How did it point to Christ?

12. Verse 36: How did the eunuch express his new faith in Christ?

13. Verses 39–40: What happened to Philip after he baptized the eunuch?

DEVOTIONAL REFLECTIONS

1. Many of us carry a great fear of persecution and death. The deaths of the martyrs should grieve believers (v. 2), and it is certainly not wrong to flee from persecution unless duty requires one to stay (v. 4). However, we must remember that those killed for Christ are immediately welcomed by Christ into glory (7:54–56). In fact, the persecution that people like Saul meant for evil God meant for good, to spread the gospel far and wide, even to Ethiopia. How does this chapter teach us to pray about persecution?

2. Though the gospel was blessed in Samaria so that many were saved, Simon shows that not every seeming conversion is real. Proper procedures of discipline must function to ensure that those who are hypocrites are unmasked and, if they refuse to repent, excluded from the membership of the church. Why can we not presume that all apparent converts are saved, even when God works powerfully in a place?

Notes

1

2

3

4

5

6

7

Notes

8

9

10

11

12

13

14

15

Notes

16

17

18

19

20

21

22

Notes

23

24

25

26

27

28

29

Notes

30

31

32

33

34

35

36

Notes

37

38

39

40

41

42

43

STUDY QUESTIONS

1. Verse 1: What does this verse tell us about Saul's character (1 Tim. 1:13)?

2. Verse 2: Why is meant by "this way" (Acts 16:17; 18:25–26; 19:9, 23; 22:4; 24:14, 22)? Why might it have been called that (Matt. 7:13–14; John 14:6)?

3. Verse 4: How could Christ say that Saul was persecuting "me" (cf. Matt. 25:40; 1 Cor. 6:15–17)?

4. Verses 8–9: What might Saul's blindness suggest about his spiritual condition?

5. Verses 15–16: What did Christ say about Saul's calling and mission?

6. Verses 19–20: What did Saul do immediately after his conversion?

7. Verse 22: What did Saul aim to prove? How did he prove it (Acts 17:2–3; 28:23)?

8. Verses 23–25: What did some Jews of Damascus plan? How did the disciples respond? Was this right (Matt. 10:23; Acts 14:6)?

9. Verses 26–27: What convinced the church in Jerusalem to receive Paul?

10. Verses 29–30: Where did the church send Paul next for his safety? Look up those places. Where are they located?

11. Verse 31: How does Luke describe the flourishing of the church in that area? How are these things connected to each other?

12. Verse 36: How is Tabitha a model of a godly woman (v. 39)?

13. Verse 39: How did these people respond to Tabitha's death? Why is that appropriate (8:2; 1 Thess. 4:13)?

14. Verses 40–42: What did Peter do when he came to the place where Tabitha's body was? What happened? What affect did it have in Joppa?

DEVOTIONAL REFLECTIONS

1. The same glory of Christ that greeted Stephen at his death (7:56) brought Saul to spiritual life (vv. 3–6). Christ is the beginning and the end of all His people's lives. Are you still living for your own glory, or has Christ's glory brought you to look away from yourself to Him? One test is whether you are willing to suffer, and even to die, so that others might see His glory. Paul was a chosen vessel specifically marked out by God to suffer for the name of Christ (v. 16). While you may not become a martyr, how willing are you to suffer some degree of insult or anger in order to make known the glory of Jesus Christ to others?

2. We do not know for how long Saul was kicking against the goads ("pricks," v. 5), but God was using His law in Paul's life to convict him of sin (Rom. 7:7–9), and no doubt Paul had heard the gospel from the very disciples he was persecuting. Are you kicking against God's goads, such as His Word, inner convictions of conscience, and works of providence that call you to Jesus? Why is it foolish to "kick against the pricks"?

3. Saul's conversion was so surprising that many doubted it could be real (v. 26). Though a period of testing is good and necessary for new converts (8:18–24), we should have high expectations of what God can do by His grace. What are the dangers of keeping true converts out of the church because of their previous lifestyles of sin?

Notes

1

2

3

4

5

6

7

8

Notes

9

10

11

12

13

14

15

16

Notes

17

18

19

20

21

22

Notes

23

24

25

26

27

28

29

Notes

30

31

32

33

34

35

36

Notes

37

38

39

40

41

42

43

Notes

44

45

46

47

48

STUDY QUESTIONS

1. Verses 1–2: What does Luke tell us about Cornelius (v. 22)?

2. Verses 5–6: What did the angel tell Cornelius to do? Why didn't the angel tell them the gospel himself (Rom. 10:14–15)?

3. Verses 9–10: What was Peter doing when he received the vision? How is that activity emphasized in this chapter (vv. 2, 4, 30–31)? Why might that be?

4. Verses 11–16: What vision and message was communicated to Peter?

5. Verse 17: How did Peter respond to the vision? What does that imply about symbolic visions in the Bible (Dan. 7:15–16)?

6. Verses 19–20: What did the Spirit do? What does this reveal about the Spirit?

7. Verse 24: What had Cornelius done while waiting for Peter to come? Why might he have done this?

8. Verses 25–26: How did Cornelius greet Peter? How did Peter respond? Why (Matt. 4:10; Acts 14:11–15; Rev. 19:10)?

9. Verse 28: What did Peter understand his vision to mean (v. 15)?

10. Verse 33: In whose presence were they? Why is that always true when we hear the preaching of the Word?

11. Verses 34–35: What does it mean to show no partiality (KJV, no respecter of persons)?

12. Verses 36–43: How would you summarize the gospel message that Peter preached?

13. Verse 39: What is the significance of Christ being hung on a "tree" or pole of wood (Deut. 21:22–23; Gal. 3:13)?

14. Verses 44–45: What happened to these Gentiles while they heard the gospel? Why were the Jews with Peter so surprised?

15. Verses 47–48: How does this verse refute the teaching that we receive the Spirit through baptism?

DEVOTIONAL REFLECTIONS

1. When considering the events of this chapter we must see them all as orchestrated by the Lord. God prepared the soil (Cornelius and his family), brought the sower of the seed (Peter), and sent down the rain (the Holy Spirit) so that there might be a harvest (conversion). All the glory goes to God and not to man. God planted a sense of need in Cornelius that made him restless and discontent with a life of paganism so that he began crying out to God in prayer. Has God awakened you to your spiritual need so that you pray for your soul and your eternal salvation? Have you embraced the gospel by the Holy Spirit?

2. Just as people had struggled with the idea that Saul of Tarsus had truly been saved, many would struggle with the concept that Gentiles like Cornelius could be saved. Our own prejudices are often so engrained that it takes a lot of convincing for us to believe what God has plainly said in His Word, that no sinner is too vile or wretched or far gone in sin for God to save him or her. What kind of people might you or others in your church have a hard time accepting if they were to be converted? Why?

Notes

Chapter 11

1

2

3

4

5

6

7

8

9

Notes

10

11

12

13

14

15

16

Notes

17

18

19

20

21

22

Notes

23

24

25

26

27

28

29

Notes

30

1. Verses 2–3: What did some Jews accuse Peter of doing? Why was this a serious matter?

2. Verses 4–17: How do these verses compare with chapter 10? Why might Luke retell the story?

3. Verses 7–8: Why was Peter disturbed by the command?

4. Verse 10: Why might the vision be repeated three times (Gen. 41:32)?

5. Verse 14: Why must people hear the gospel (Acts 4:12)?

6. Verse 18: What gift must God give if sinners will gain life (Acts 5:31; 2 Tim. 2:25)?

7. Verses 20–21: Why did the evangelism in Antioch result in conversions?

8. Verses 23–24: What does Luke tell us about the character and ministry of Barnabas?

9. Verse 26: Based on this verse, how would you define the noun "Christian"?

10. Verses 28–30: What did Agabus prophesy? How did the Antioch church respond?

DEVOTIONAL REFLECTIONS

1. Peter's vision did not introduce the idea of the inclusion of the Gentiles into salvation, nor did it inaugurate this change. It was prophesied in the Old Testament (Ps. 72:17–19), foretold by Jesus (Luke 24:44–47), and accomplished by His death (Eph. 2:12–15). The vision of Peter confirmed the change and prodded the church to follow Christ in evangelizing and welcoming the nations. Why are we sometimes slow to take the gospel to ethnic groups or cultures that are different from our own? Why does the Lord press us to do so?

2. Barnabas visited the believers in Antioch and saw "the grace of God" in the work there (v. 23). This means that he saw the results of the grace of God at work in the lives of those who had come to trust in Christ and follow Him as His disciples. The name "Christians" was first used of believers and disciples in Antioch (v. 26); the name expresses the close relationship between Christ, which means "Anointed One," and His people who share His anointing in the Holy Spirit. If we carry the name of "Christian," why is it important that people be able to see the grace of Christ's Spirit in our lives?

Notes

Chapter 12

1

2

3

4

5

6

7

Notes

8

9

10

11

12

13

Notes

14

15

16

17

18

19

Notes

20

21

22

23

24

25

STUDY QUESTIONS

1. Verses 1–4: What actions were taken by Herod (Agrippa I), grand-son of Herod the Great?

2. Verse 5: How did the church respond to this crisis?

3. Verses 6–10: What did the angel do? How does this show us the power of angels?

4. Verse 12: What were many believers doing in this house? Why (Matt. 18:19)?

5. Verses 13–16: How do we see the foolishness and spiritual weakness of believers here?

6. Verse 17: If James, the brother of John, had been killed by Herod (v. 2), what James was this (Matt. 13:55; Gal. 1:19; 2:9)?

7. Verse 23: What did God's angel do to Herod? Why? What warning does this give to proud persecutors?

8. Verse 24: What did God cause to happen with His word, even under persecution?

DEVOTIONAL REFLECTIONS

1. Why James was killed and Peter was allowed to live for several more years is a divine mystery. God could have supernaturally saved both James and Peter. He showed His sovereignty in allowing Peter to do more work on earth, while James would enter Christ's presence sooner. When we are tempted to compare our circumstances in life with those of others, how can what happened to James and Peter teach us to submit to God?

2. Jesus commands His disciples to continually ask, seek, and knock for their requests, anticipating that God will hear our prayers. Thus the scene before us in this chapter is so striking: when their prayers were answered they could not believe it. Even as we pray for various requests, we should also pray, "Lord, increase our faith" (Luke 17:5).

3. Their deaths are recorded in the same chapter of the Bible, but what different deaths James and Herod experienced! In one moment James went from prison to heaven. Herod, too, in one moment went from his earthly glory to an everlasting prison in hell. How true it is: "Blessed are the dead which die in the Lord" (Rev. 14:13).

Notes

1

2

3

4

5

6

7

Notes

8

9

10

11

12

13

Notes

14

15

16

17

18

19

20

Notes

21

22

23

24

25

26

Notes

27

28

29

30

31

32

33

Notes

34

35

36

37

38

39

40

Notes

41

42

43

44

45

46

Notes

47

48

49

50

51

52

STUDY QUESTIONS

1. Verses 2–4: What did the Holy Spirit do? What does this teach us about the Holy Spirit?

2. Verse 6: Who was this Bar-Jesus?

3. Verse 8: What did he do when Paul was evangelizing the civil ruler of the region?

4. Verses 10–12: What did the Holy Spirit fill Paul to say and do to this sorcerer? How did that affect the civil ruler who witnessed it?

5. Verses 14–15: How did Paul start his mission in Antioch of Pisidia? Why (Rom. 1:16)?

6. Verses 17–22: How did Paul begin his sermon? Why begin this way when preaching Jesus Christ in a Jewish synagogue?

7. Verse 23: What promise did God give David that is fulfilled in Jesus (2 Sam. 7:12–14; Ps. 132:11)?

8. Verses 24–25: How did John prepare Israel for Christ?

9. Verse 26: To what two groups did Paul preach the gospel of salvation (v. 16)?

10. Verses 27–31: How do these verses compare to Paul's gospel summary in 1 Corinthians 15:3–5?

11. Verses 32–37: How did Paul prove from Scripture that Jesus is the promised one?

12. Verses 38–39: What did Paul offer them in Jesus Christ?

13. Verses 40–41: What warning did Paul give?

14. Verse 43: How did Paul and Barnabas counsel those who received their teaching?

15. Verse 45: Why did the Jews turn against Paul?

16. Verse 46: What were the unbelieving Jews rejecting?

17. Verse 48: Why do some believe the gospel, when others do not?

18. Verse 51: What symbolic action did Paul and Barnabas do in response to those who persecuted them? What does it mean (Neh. 5:13; Matt. 10:14–15)?

19. Verse 52: What was true of the disciples, despite, or perhaps because of, their suffering persecution?

DEVOTIONAL REFLECTIONS

1. Though the Holy Spirit sent Paul and Barnabas to preach the gospel to the lost, the church in Antioch was the vehicle through which the Spirit set them apart for this ministry. Do you pray for missionaries and support them as you are able?

2. Paul met many enemies of the gospel on his journey, the sorcerer Bar-Jesus being only one of them. Christ's promise that the gates of hell cannot prevail against the church is profoundly meaningful in the midst of such hellish conflict (Matt. 16:18). Why do we need to be filled with the power of God's Spirit to see the kingdom advance?

3. When they heard the stunning message of free justification by faith alone, some wanted to hear this exact message preached again on the next Sabbath (v. 42). What a blessed thing it is never to tire of the "old" gospel, to find it always new. What do we learn about the content of the gospel message from this chapter? What makes it so precious?

Notes

Chapter 14

1

2

3

4

5

6

7

Notes

8

9

10

11

12

13

14

Notes

15

16

17

18

19

20

21

Notes

22

23

24

25

26

27

28

STUDY QUESTIONS

1. Verses 1–3: How does Luke describe the ministry of Paul and Barnabas, and the response by Jews and Gentiles?

2. Verses 5–6: What prompted the missionaries to flee the city?

3. Verses 9–10: Why did Paul heal this particular crippled man?

4. Verses 11–13: How did the people misinterpret the meaning of the miracle? How does this event illustrate the need for teaching, and not just works, in evangelism?

5. Verses 14–18: How did the missionaries correct this misunderstanding? What does this teach about God's general revelation of himself to mankind (Rom. 1:19–21)?

6. Verse 19: What did the Jews from Antioch and Iconium do?

7. Verses 20–21: What did Paul do after being stoned by a mob? What does this show us about him?

8. Verses 22–23: How did the missionaries help the new disciples and churches?

9. Verse 27: What did the missionaries do when they came to their home church? To whom did they give glory for the faith of the new believers?

DEVOTIONAL REFLECTIONS

1. Imagine seeing Paul when he returned to Lystra, perhaps with bruises and cuts from being stoned still visible on him from when he was last there. What would it have been like to hear this man say, "we must through much tribulation enter into the kingdom of God" (v. 22)? What might it cost a typical Christian in your land to follow Christ to the end? What has it cost you?

2. This section on Paul's first missionary journey (13:1–14:28) concludes with a concern for proper church order. Paul and Barnabas prayerfully led each church to appoint a group of elders to lead it. The missionaries returned to their sending church to report about God's work through them among the nations. There is a profound sense that both office-bearers in the church and missionaries from the church serve as those commissioned by the church and upheld by its prayers. Why is the local church central to world missions?

Notes

Chapter 15

1

2

3

4

5

6

Notes

7

8

9

10

11

12

13

Notes

14

15

16

17

18

19

20

21

Notes

22

23

24

25

26

27

Notes

28

29

30

31

32

33

34

35

Notes

36

37

38

39

40

41

STUDY QUESTIONS

1. Verse 1: What did these people from Judea say about circumcision (v. 5)?

2. Verses 2–4: What two actions did Paul and Barnabas take in conjunction with the church in Antioch?

3. Verse 9: What does God work in the heart by faith (1 Peter 1:22)?

4. Verse 11: How is anyone—whether Jew or Gentile—saved (Eph. 2:5, 8)?

5. Verses 16–18: What passage of Scripture did James quote? What does it say about the Gentiles?

6. Verses 19–21: What did James propose as a solution for this controversy?

7. Verses 22–23: Who does Luke say issued this decree?

8. Verses 25–26: How did they commend Barnabas and Paul?

9. Verse 28: Who supervised the meeting and its decision?

10. Verse 29: Why were these prohibitions important for the unity of Jews and Gentiles in Christ?

11. Verses 30–33: How did the church in Antioch receive the letter (KJV, epistle)?

12. Verses 37–41: How does Luke describe the disagreement over Mark? Was this a permanent breach between Paul and Mark (Col. 4:10; 2 Tim. 4:11; Philemon 24)?

DEVOTIONAL REFLECTIONS

1. The early church had to contend not only with persecution but also with strife and division. We can learn important principles from how the church in Jerusalem responded. First, the leaders of the church met together to discuss the matter. Second, their discussion was God-centered and God-exalting; together they looked to His will and bowed to His providence. Third, they discussed the Holy Scriptures, basing their decision on the Spirit's teaching in the Word of God. Fourth, they guided their decision by the principles of salvation by grace through faith in Jesus Christ, not through bondage to human traditions or old covenant ceremonies. Fifth, no one man decreed what the church would do; though Peter and James had more authority than the others, the church sought unity of mind. How can your church put these lessons into practice in its own discussions?

2. Another interesting disagreement, this time of a personal nature, is recorded here between Barnabas and Paul (vv. 37–39). This one was solved by the two going their separate ways. Another way of looking at this was that now two teams went out, doubling the effectiveness and coverage of the mission effort. Even this conflict could not halt the work of God. Is it ever necessary for two Christians who share common beliefs nevertheless to go separate ways in ministry? Why?

Notes

1

2

3

4

5

6

Notes

7

8

9

10

11

12

13

Notes

14

15

16

17

18

Notes

19

20

21

22

23

24

25

Notes

26

27

28

29

30

31

32

33

Notes

34

35

36

37

38

39

40

1. Verses 1–2: What were Timothy's background and character (2 Tim. 1:5; 3:15)?

2. Verses 4–5: What effect did the decree by the apostles and elders in Jerusalem have on these other churches?

3. Verses 6–7: Why did Paul's missionary team not go to Asia Minor or Bithynia? What do these verses imply about the Holy Spirit?

4. Verse 10: What does the "we" imply about the author of Acts (vv. 11, 15, 17)?

5. Verses 14–15: Why did Lydia listen attentively and come to faith in Christ?

6. Verses 16–19: Why did the owners of the slave girl persecute Paul and Silas?

7. Verses 20–21: What accusation did they bring against the Christian missionaries?

8. Verses 22–25: How were Paul and Silas treated? How did they respond?

9. Verse 27: Why was the jailer going to kill himself?

10. Verse 30: What did the jailer ask Paul and Silas? What factors might have brought him to ask this question?

11. Verses 31–34: What do these verses say about the jailer's household?

12. Verses 35–37: What message did the magistrates send concerning Paul and Silas? How did Paul respond? Why might he have done that?

13. Verse 38: What is the significance of their being Roman citizens (Acts 22:25–29)?

DEVOTIONAL REFLECTIONS

1. The Holy Spirit is an integral part of the church's mission. Here we read of the Spirit both forbidding and permitting Paul and his companions to carry out their ministry (vv. 6–7). Though today we seek no revelations of the Spirit apart from the Scriptures, we do need to rely upon Him for wisdom in every decision regarding church and evangelism. Furthermore, the opening of Lydia's heart to believe (v. 14) reminds us that the preaching of the gospel depends completely on the Spirit for success in conversions. How should these realities motivate us to pray? How do you pray with regard to these matters?

2. With the earthquake and the outstretched sword, the conversion of the jailor was violent and forceful, but no less productive of true faith and joy (v. 34) than that of Lydia. God's actions in bringing people to Christ are different for each person, but true, saving grace always shows itself in faith and love that God Himself works in the hearts of sinners. Why is it a mistake to insist that each person's experience of conversion has exactly the same outward features?

Notes

Chapter 17

1

2

3

4

5

6

Notes

7

8

9

10

11

12

13

Notes

14

15

16

17

18

19

Notes

20

21

22

23

24

25

26

Notes

27

28

29

30

31

32

33

Notes

34

STUDY QUESTIONS

1. Verses 1–3: What was Paul's normal method of evangelism (Acts 18:4)?

2. Verse 5: What motivated men to stir up an angry mob (Matt. 27:18; Acts 13:45)?

3. Verses 6–7: What dangerous charges did they make against the Christians?

4. Verse 11: What noble thing did the Berean Jews do?

5. Verse 16: What provoked Paul in Athens?

6. Verse 18: How did Greek philosophers react to the gospel?

7. Verse 21: What did these Greeks love about philosophy?

8. Verses 24–26: How did Paul describe the true God?

9. Verses 28–29: How did Paul use a pagan writer to critique pagan ideas?

10. Verse 30: What does God command as the proper response to the gospel?

11. Verse 31: What does Christ's resurrection show?

DEVOTIONAL REFLECTIONS

1. The Bereans serve as a good example of men and women who love truth and the Scriptures. After hearing the preaching and teaching of the apostles, they "received the word with all readiness of mind, and searched the scriptures daily, whether those things were so" (v. 11). So often we fall into a passive kind of sitting under the teaching and preaching of the Word. The Bereans are commended for their eagerness to search the Scriptures and discover the truth of the apostles' teaching. How can we imitate them?

2. Paul's preaching to those who knew the Scriptures (v. 2) and those steeped in worldly philosophy (vv. 16–31) was different. However, Paul's message in the Areopagus has sometimes been misapplied, as though Paul were using this opportunity to build bridges of common beliefs between Christianity and different religions and philosophies. On the contrary, Paul's message was as sharp as ever, exposing sin, idolatry, and ignorance; declaring the glory of the true God and Savior; and calling men to repent now or face the judgment. What can we learn from him for speaking about our faith to people outside the church?

Notes

Chapter 18

1

2

3

4

5

6

7

Notes

8

9

10

11

12

13

14

15

Notes

16

17

18

19

20

21

22

Notes

23

24

25

26

27

28

STUDY QUESTIONS

1. Verse 2: Who were Aquila and Priscilla (v. 18; Rom. 16:3–5; 1 Cor. 16:19; 2 Tim. 4:19)?

2. Verse 3: How did Paul make a living?

3. Verse 8: How did the household of Crispus respond to the gospel?

4. Verses 9–10: How did the Lord encourage Paul?

5. Verses 14–16: Why didn't Paul need to defend himself in this court?

6. Verse 17: What do we see here about the character of Gallio, the ruler of Achaia (v. 12)?

7. Verse 21: What did Paul say his return to see them again depended on?

8. Verses 24–28: How is Apollos a model for preachers?

DEVOTIONAL REFLECTIONS

1. Even Paul could feel afraid (v. 9). Christ encouraged Paul during the difficult early stage of his time in Corinth. He was working hard making tents for a living (v. 3), and his witness was opposed (v. 6). However, God's works are known to Him from all eternity. He tells Paul that He has "much people in this city" (v. 10). That did not mean that there had been many converts to this point but that Christ had claimed them as His own by the decree of election. They still needed the preaching of the gospel so that they might come to faith and repentance and thereby confirm their election from God (1 Thess. 1:3–6). How does the truth that God has chosen many sinners for salvation encourage evangelism?

2. Apollos was "mighty in the scriptures" (v. 24). No doubt that meant that by the Spirit's grace he loved the Bible, studied it carefully, and could teach it well (Ezra 7:10). It was like a sword that he used to defend the truth, attack strongholds of unbelief, and set prisoners free. His response to Aquila and Priscilla shows that he was still humble, teachable, and eager to grow in his knowledge (v. 26). How can we imitate his example?

Notes

1

2

3

4

5

6

7

8

Notes

9

10

11

12

13

14

15

Notes

16

17

18

19

20

21

22

Notes

23

24

25

26

27

28

Notes

29

30

31

32

33

34

Notes

35

36

37

38

39

40

41

STUDY QUESTIONS

1. Verses 1–2: What did these disciples lack?

2. Verses 3–5: What baptism had they received? What baptism did they need to receive?

3. Verses 8–9: Why did Paul separate the disciples from the synagogue?

4. Verses 11–12: What kinds of miracles was God working through Paul?

5. Verses 13–17: What happened to the sons of Sceva? What effect did that have on others?

6. Verses 18–20: What did the people who had been practicing magic (KJV, curious arts) do when they believed and repented? How did that affect the ministry of God's Word?

7. Verse 21: What did Paul resolve to do?

8. Verses 24–28: What does this incident teach us about the motives that can lie behind the religious persecution of Christians?

9. Verse 29: What resulted from the anger of the silversmiths against the missionaries?

10. Verses 30–31: What did Paul's fellow disciples and friends urge him to do? Why was that wise and good?

11. Verse 32: What danger of mob action is evident here?

12. Verses 35–37: How did God use this unbelieving official to protect his church?

13. Verses 38–41: What did the official counsel the crowd to do? How does law and order in society help the church?

DEVOTIONAL REFLECTIONS

1. The advance of the gospel faces many obstacles and enemies. There is incomplete knowledge, a situation in which people know enough to call themselves disciples but lack a full understanding of the gospel and thus also lack spiritual power. There is hardness of heart, whereby the very people one expects to welcome the gospel force the church to separate from them. There is magic and sorcery, which may even try to use "Jesus" as another spiritual force to invoke without knowing the Lord. There is idolatry so deeply embedded in society that it drives the economy. There is persecution that can threaten the lives of Christians with violent mobs. Nevertheless we read, "So mightily grew the word of God and prevailed" (v. 20). God's Word carries God's power to accomplish God's purposes. How can that encourage those who preach and teach the Bible?

2. Materialism is a false god that must be renounced if we are to follow Christ. For the Ephesians, repentance required destroying books of sorcery that had cost an enormous amount of money (v. 19), but the Christians took the loss in order to honor Christ. On the other hand, the love of money turned the silversmiths into violent enemies of the church, even though they pretended to act in religious zeal (vv. 25–31). What place does money hold in your heart relative to Christ? How do you know?

Notes

1

2

3

4

5

6

7

Notes

8

9

10

11

12

13

14

Notes

15

16

17

18

19

20

21

Notes

22

23

24

25

26

27

28

29

Notes

30

31

32

33

34

35

36

Notes

37

38

STUDY QUESTIONS

1. Verse 3: Why did Paul change his travel plans?

2. Verse 7: What does this verse suggest about the worship of the apostolic church?

3. Verses 8–12: What happened to Eutychus? How does this miracle glorify God?

4. Verse 11: Why did Paul stay up all night with them?

5. Verses 13–15: What do "we" and "us" in this passage imply about the author of Acts?

6. Verse 17: Whom did Paul call to meet with him?

7. Verses 19–21: How is Paul a model of a godly elder in his conduct and teaching?

8. Verses 22–24: What did Paul treasure? What did he not treasure?

9. Verses 26–27: What did Paul say here? What does that mean (Ezek. 33:7–9)?

10. Verses 28–31: What is the calling of elders (including ministers of the Word)?

11. Verse 32: What equips elders to fulfill their calling?

12. Verses 33–35: How is Paul a model of a godly elder in his handling of money?

13. Verses 36–38: How did Paul and the elders end their meeting with each other? What can we learn from this about the relationships between godly leaders?

DEVOTIONAL REFLECTIONS

1. Paul's ministry did not hold back anything that would truly profit his people (v. 20). He imparted to them the whole counsel of God (v. 27) from beginning to end, for all God's truth is profitable (2 Tim. 3:16). He did not skip over difficult doctrines or hard sayings, nor did he leave out sweet comforts and encouraging exhortations. We may be tempted to be imbalanced and to avoid certain teachings of Scripture, but this comes from pride and self-love instead of serving in love for God and our neighbor. In contrast, Paul did not love his own life but gave his complete devotion to being faithful to the Word. How is he an example for pastors and teachers? How is he an example for us all?

2. Paul was concerned about "grievous wolves" entering the flock and not sparing it (v. 29). Though God will save His elect from damnation and Christ will preserve His church on earth, local congregations and even groups of churches can be ruined by false teaching. Therefore we must guard against it and encourage our elders to do the same. Why is it difficult to oppose false teachers? Why is it crucial?

Notes

1

2

3

4

5

6

Notes

7

8

9

10

11

12

13

Notes

14

15

16

17

18

19

20

Notes

21

22

23

24

25

Notes

26

27

28

29

30

31

Notes

32

33

34

35

36

37

38

Notes

39

40

STUDY QUESTIONS

1. Verse 4: What advice were the disciples giving Paul? How was the Holy Spirit involved (Acts 20:23)?

2. Verse 5: What did the disciples at Tyre do with the missionaries before they left?

3. Verses 8–9: What do we learn about Philip in this passage?

4. Verse 11: When a prophet prophesied, who was speaking?

5. Verse 13: Why was Paul willing to die?

6. Verse 17: How did the Jerusalem church treat Paul?

7. Verses 18–21: How did James and the elders at Jerusalem respond to Paul's visit and missionary report?

8. Verses 23–24: What vow had these men taken? What expenses would Paul pay for them (Num. 6:1–21)?

9. Verse 26: Why was Paul willing to observe Old Testament ceremonies (1 Cor. 9:19–20)?

10. Verses 27–29: What did these Jews from Asia do? How does this illustrate the danger of making assumptions about other people?

11. Verse 32: How did the arrival of the Roman soldiers change how the Jews were treating Paul?

12. Verses 34, 38: How was this situation full of confusion?

13. Verses 37, 40: What language did Paul speak to the Roman soldier? To the crowd of Jews? Why was Paul's knowledge of both languages helpful (Acts 22:2)?

DEVOTIONAL REFLECTIONS

1. What a beautiful prayer meeting on the shore (v. 5). Do you think the children, at least the older ones, ever forgot kneeling there with the apostle Paul as he was heading to Jerusalem to suffer for the gospel's sake? Why is it good to send off friends with prayer?

2. Mnason of Cyprus, known as "an old disciple," opened his house to Paul (v. 16). What are the blessings of following Christ for a long time into old age? They must have enjoyed sweet fellowship in Mnason's home. What blessings does it bring to show hospitality to traveling missionaries and pastors?

3. As in the riot in Ephesus (19:29–41), the mob in Jerusalem was full of confusion (21:30–34), acting rashly in violence on the basis of false information (vv. 28–29). Why is it foolish to join an angry mob? What is a better alternative for addressing wrongs?

Notes

Chapter 22

1

2

3

4

5

6

Notes

7

8

9

10

11

12

13

Notes

14

15

16

17

18

19

20

21

Notes

22

23

24

25

26

27

28

Notes

29

30

1. Verse 1: How does this chapter compare to chapters 9 and 26? Why might Luke have done this when composing this book?

2. Verses 3–5: How did Paul describe his life before he encountered Christ?

3. Verses 6–7, 11: How did the glory of Christ affect Saul?

4. Verse 12: How did Paul describe Ananias?

5. Verses 14–15: Why did God save Paul?

6. Verses 17–18: What did Christ reveal to Paul on a previous visit to Jerusalem?

7. Verses 21–23: What did Paul say that provoked the Jews to erupt in rage?

8. Verse 24: What were the Roman soldiers preparing to do to Paul? What would that involve (look up "scourge" in a dictionary or encyclopedia)?

9. Verses 25–29: How did Paul use his Roman citizenship to protect himself?

10. Verse 30: Why was Paul brought before the Jewish council?

DEVOTIONAL REFLECTIONS

1. When God converts us, even if we are in a crowd, it is as though He leads us apart and speaks to us personally. His words enter our minds and hearts in a way that may leave others untouched and cold. Conversion is God's sovereign work in the individual soul. It glorifies Him for us to reflect upon our conversions, whether dramatic or quiet, and to tell others of the work of our Savior. Has God saved you? If so, how does your conversion manifest the glory of His sovereign grace?

2. Paul loved those who were his people according to the flesh. He would have died for his fellow Jews if this would have saved them (Rom. 9:1–3). Even after they unjustly seized him and beat him he did not curse them but lovingly told them about the Savior of both Jew and Gentile. Do you have a burden for those who do not know Christ? What can you do with that burden?

Notes

1

2

3

4

5

6

7

Notes

8

9

10

11

12

13

Notes

14

15

16

17

18

19

Notes

20

21

22

23

24

25

26

Notes

27

28

29

30

31

32

33

Notes

34

35

1. Verse 1: How does Paul describe his life as a Christian (Acts 24:16)? What does this mean (Heb. 9:14; 13:18)?

2. Verse 3: What did Paul mean by calling him a whitewashed wall (Matt. 23:27)?

3. Verses 6–9: How did Paul divide the council?

4. Verse 11: What promise did Christ give to Paul?

5. Verses 12–13: What grave danger threatened to nullify Christ's promise?

6. Verses 16–22: How did the Lord use a young man to rescue Paul?

7. Verses 23–24: How did the Lord use the Roman army to protect Paul?

8. Verse 26: What was the captain's name? Why might Luke have told us this?

9. Verse 29: How would this statement vindicate persecuted Christians?

10. Verse 33: Where did they bring Paul? (If you can, locate this city on a map and write down where it is relative to Jerusalem.)

DEVOTIONAL REFLECTIONS

1. Paul was in prison for the hope of Israel. Already a Pharisee, he had believed there was such a thing as a resurrection, though he did not believe that Christ had been raised until He appeared to him on the road to Damascus. It was then that he came to understand that Christ fulfilled Old Testament prophecy and that Jesus Himself was the hope of Israel. Jeremiah called God Himself "the hope of Israel" (Jer. 14:8; 17:13), and when Paul met Christ he lost all hope in himself and saw Christ as his only hope. Why is the future resurrection that Christ will bring the center of the hope of believers?

2. Christ appeared to Paul to assure him that he would testify not only in Jerusalem but also in Rome (v. 11). Paul's work was not yet done. Even though people plotted his death day and night, Christ's word could not be undone. God predestined not only the sufferings of His Son to purchase redemption but also the success of His servants to proclaim redemption so that the nations would believe. While we do not know God's specific decree for our future, how can recognizing His sovereignty give us confidence in serving Him?

Notes

1

2

3

4

5

6

7

Notes

8

9

10

11

12

13

14

Notes

15

16

17

18

19

20

21

Notes

22

23

24

25

26

27

STUDY QUESTIONS

1. Verses 2–3: What was the character of Antonius Felix (check an encyclopedia or Bible dictionary)?

2. Verses 5–6: What were the charges against Paul? Were they true?

3. Verses 11–13: What was Paul's defense?

4. Verse 14: What did Paul confess about Christianity ("the way")?

5. Verse 15: What was the ancient hope of Israel?

6. Verses 18–19: How else did Paul defend himself?

7. Verse 21: What did Paul say was the heart of the controversy?

8. Verses 24–25: How did Luke describe Paul's evangelization of Felix and Drusilla, and its effect?

9. Verses 26–27: What were Felix's motives in keeping Paul in prison?

DEVOTIONAL REFLECTIONS

1. Paul held before all his hearers the truth of the resurrection of the dead, "both of the just and unjust" (v. 15). It is a solemn truth that we will rise again, and all souls that ever lived will be in one or the other group: righteous or wicked. Felix trembled when he heard of "righteousness, temperance, and judgment to come" (v. 25), but he did not repent. Why is it not enough to feel guilt over sin and fear over the judgment day? What did Felix lack in order to be saved?

2. One reason Paul could speak so boldly and freely before all men when Felix trembled before God was that Paul's mindset was "to have always a conscience void to offence toward God, and toward men" (v. 16). Proverbs 28:1 says, "The wicked flee when no man pursueth: but the righteous are bold as a lion." Obviously Paul was a sinner, but he sought daily cleansing for his sins and grace to live righteously and holily by grace. Why does living with a clear conscience give courage? How can we do this?

Notes

1

2

3

4

5

6

7

Notes

8

9

10

11

12

13

Notes

14

15

16

17

18

19

Notes

20

21

22

23

24

25

Notes

26

27

STUDY QUESTIONS

1. Verses 1–3: What danger again threatened Paul?

2. Verse 7: What does Luke tell us about the accusations against Paul?

3. Verses 10–12: How did Paul respond when the Jews desired to judge him in Jerusalem? Why might he have done that (Acts 19:21; 23:11; 25:21)?

4. Verse 13: Who were Agrippa (King Herod Agrippa II) and Bernice (check an encyclopedia or Bible dictionary)?

5. Verse 16: Why didn't Festus hand Paul over to the Jewish leaders to be put to death? How does this illustrate the importance of a good legal system?

6. Verses 18–19: How did Festus summarize Paul's case?

7. Verse 23: How would you describe this scene as it appeared to human eyes? From a spiritual perspective, how was it an opportunity for evangelism?

8. Verses 26–27: Why did Festus ask Agrippa to hear Paul?

DEVOTIONAL REFLECTIONS

1. Though Paul was in prison for the sake of the gospel, the word of God was not bound. Paul's sorrows became doorways for the gospel to come to rulers and judges. Though they came in great pomp and show of their power and wealth, they were desperately needy sinners who would soon face death, after which would come judgment. When persecution brings God's people before rulers and judges, let us remember that the Lord Jesus rules over all for the sake of spreading the gospel to all people. How should this change the way we view our trials? In what way should it make us alert for evangelistic opportunities?

2. Paul's accusers had many and grievous complaints against Paul, but "they could not prove" them (v. 7). Christ's faithful servants mirror the righteousness of their Lord, although imperfectly, and thus even the world must admit that they have done nothing worthy of the persecution they endure. If you were brought to trial before men, could they find you guilty of no other crime than being a faithful Christian?

Notes

1

2

3

4

5

6

7

Notes

8

9

10

11

12

13

14

Notes

15

16

17

18

19

20

21

Notes

22

23

24

25

26

27

28

Notes

29

30

31

32

STUDY QUESTIONS

1. Verse 3: What especially qualified Agrippa to hear Paul's case?

2. Verse 5: What was Paul's religious background (Phil. 3:4–6)?

3. Verses 6–8: What did Paul say was the real reason for his trial?

4. Verses 9–11: What was the motive and method of Paul's persecution of the church?

5. Verses 13–15: What can we learn from this passage about Christ?

6. Verse 18: How does this verse offer a summary of true conversion?

7. Verse 20: What is the gospel's command to all nations?

8. Verse 22: How does Paul's gospel compare to the message of the Old Testament?

9. Verse 23: How does this verse offer a summary of the gospel (Luke 24:45–47)?

10. Verse 29: What did Paul desire for all who heard him?

11. Verse 31: What verdict did Festus, Agrippa, and Bernice reach?

DEVOTIONAL REFLECTIONS

1. Verse 18 gives us a short but rich summary of the true conversion Christ works through the preaching of the gospel. What does this verse teach us about the nature of conversion? What does it teach about its happy effects?

2. Agrippa knew much about the Scriptures (v. 3), being an expert in all sorts of matters relating to the Jews. He is said to have believed the prophets (v. 27), which means he must have given intellectual assent to the Bible. Nevertheless, he would not bow under the Christ of the Scriptures. Yet he said, "Almost thou persuadest me" (v. 28). He remained tragically blind, unrepentantly clinging to sin and remaining a part of the kingdom of Satan (v. 18). "Almost Christians" end up in hell. Only those who submit entirely to the righteousness of God in Christ, abandoning all hope of being saved by any other means, will be saved. What might it look like to be an "almost Christian" today? What does this text say to such people?

Notes

Chapter 27

1

2

3

4

5

6

Notes

7

8

9

10

11

12

Notes

13

14

15

16

17

18

19

Notes

20

21

22

23

24

25

26

Notes

27

28

29

30

31

32

Notes

33

34

35

36

37

38

39

40

41

42

43

44

STUDY QUESTIONS

1. Verse 1: Who was the Roman centurion in charge of Paul and the other prisoners?

2. Verse 3: How was Paul treated by the centurion?

3. Verses 4, 7: What slowed their voyage?

4. Verses 9–12: What did Paul perceive about their plan to sail?

5. Verses 14–20: What did they experience during this storm? How would you have felt?

6. Verses 21–26: What had the Lord revealed to Paul through an angel?

7. Verse 27: How long had they been at sea at this point?

8. Verse 28: What is a fathom? What would the depths be in feet or meters?

9. Verse 30: What were the sailors attempting to do?

10. Verse 31: What did Paul tell the soldiers? How can this be true if God promised the safety of all on board?

11. Verses 33–36: What did Paul urge them to do? How did Paul, the prisoner, become as a leader to them all?

12. Verse 37: How many people were exposed to Paul's life and gospel during this crisis?

13. Verses 42–43: How was Paul's life spared again?

14. Verse 44: How many of those aboard the ship came safely to land? What does this reveal about God's faithfulness and mercy?

DEVOTIONAL REFLECTIONS

1. We need to be careful not to draw conclusions from providence. "Fair weather" providences do not mean that it is always good to move ahead as we plan. Nor do "stormy" providences necessarily mean we are doomed to fail. Our faith and duty must not take their direction from the shifting winds of providence but from the unchanging promises of God. Why is it dangerous to take today's providence as tomorrow's promise?

2. On this ship Paul was strikingly unlike Jonah, the Old Testament prophet who followed the path of disobedience. In that situation the sailors almost lost their lives because of him (Jonah 1:6); now the sailors were saved because of Paul (v. 24). Jonah hid, sleeping, below deck until the pagan sailors roused him, but Paul gave leadership and encouragement through his words and prayers. When trials come, how are we tempted to be like Jonah? How ought we to be like Paul?

3. The church of Christ sometimes seems doomed to sink beneath the waves of its troubles, but the Lord Jesus still rules the seas. Paul's troubles in the ship seemed to threaten his mission to Rome but instead proved to be an opportunity to demonstrate God's power and love to 276 people in a way they would never forget. How can that encourage the church in its mission to the world?

Notes

1

2

3

4

5

6

Notes

7

8

9

10

11

12

13

Notes

14

15

16

17

18

Notes

19

20

21

22

23

24

Notes

25

26

27

28

29

30

31

1. Verse 2: How did the people of the island treat the survivors of the shipwreck?

2. Verses 4–6: How did the people's pagan mindset distort how they viewed Paul?

3. Verses 8–9: How did God reveal His mercy to the people?

4. Verse 11: What images did the ship bear? Why?

5. Verse 15: What encouraged Paul when he neared Rome?

6. Verse 16: What liberty was Paul granted in Rome?

7. Verse 20: To what cause did Paul attribute his being chained?

8. Verse 22: What had the Jews in Rome heard about Christianity?

9. Verse 23: How does Luke describe Paul's teaching in Rome?

10. Verses 26–27: What Old Testament passage did Paul quote? What does it mean?

11. Verses 30–31: How does the book of Acts end? How does this passage summarize a major theme of the book?

DEVOTIONAL REFLECTIONS

The Gospel of Luke started in rural Judaea, after the emperor had compelled the people to register for taxes, unwittingly bringing the unborn Christ to the place where the Scriptures had foretold His birth. The book of Acts ends in the heart of the Roman Empire, with God's servant boldly preaching Christ and His kingdom in the city of Caesar. From beginning to end the writings of Luke testify that God is fulfilling His decree concerning the Savior. Nothing could stop the complete accomplishment of redemption by Christ's death and resurrection, and nothing can stop the preaching of the gospel to all nations—not even a poisonous snakebite on a missionary's hand. It is not pagan gods or luck that rules over this world but the triune God. This does not permit us to be foolish or fail to use God's appointed means, but it does teach us to serve Christ with confidence. How does the closing scene of Acts encourage you about the future of the kingdom of Jesus Christ? What is your standing in relationship to Christ and His kingdom?